# RAND NATIONAL SECURITY RESEARCH DIVISION

T0097351

# Preparing North Korean Elites for Unification

Bruce W. Bennett

Prepared for the Korea Foundation

For more information on this publication, visit www.rand.org/t/RR1985

**Library of Congress Cataloging-in-Publication Data** is available for this publication.
ISBN: 978-0-8330-9798-9

Published by the RAND Corporation, Santa Monica, Calif.
© Copyright 2017 RAND Corporation
**RAND**® is a registered trademark.

*Cover images from iStock/gettyimages*

### Support RAND
Make a tax-deductible charitable contribution at
www.rand.org/giving/contribute

www.rand.org

# Preface

Korean unification is a major issue in the Republic of Korea (ROK, also known as South Korea). But North Korean propaganda indoctrinates North Korean elites to believe that an ROK-led unification would be a disaster for them. Successful unification will likely require that North Korean elites feel the unification will in fact be good for them. This report identifies the likely concerns of North Korean elites about their futures and fates under various unification scenarios and recommends actions that the ROK can take now to help North Korean elites feel more positive about, or at least less resistant to, unification.

This research was sponsored by the Korea Foundation and conducted within the International Security and Defense Policy (ISDP) Center of the RAND National Security Research Division (NSRD). NSRD conducts research and analysis on defense and national security topics for the U.S. and allied defense, foreign policy, homeland security, and intelligence communities and foundations and other nongovernmental organizations that support defense and national security analysis.

For more information on the RAND International Security and Defense Policy Center, see www.rand.org/nsrd/ndri/centers/isdp or contact the director (contact information is provided on the web page).

# Contents

# Figures

# Summary

Korean unification is a major issue in the Republic of Korea (ROK, also known as South Korea). Many in the ROK believe that because their country significantly dominates North Korea in economic, demographic, and world stature terms, any unification will be led by the South. Because the ROK would not be able to trust many North Korean elites, these elites would likely be subjected to transitional justice and disenfranchisement. North Korean indoctrination efforts have capitalized on this probable development, making the case that ROK-led unification would be a disaster for North Korean elites, and have used this fear to bind elites closer to the regime and make them more hostile to ROK-led unification. It is therefore very hard to imagine that North Korean elites would agree to a peaceful unification absent a change in messaging from the South. And if Korean unification is somehow imposed on the North, perhaps as the result of a failed North Korean invasion of the ROK, many North Korean elites would likely support serious resistance against a unified Korean government—resistance that would, at a minimum, make unification protracted and even more costly than it is already likely to be; at worst, such resistance could even cause Korean unification to fail.

For Korean unification to succeed, North Korean elites likely need to feel that unification will be good for them, or at least not unacceptably bad. This report identifies five concerns that North Korean elites would likely have relative to unification: individual safety and security, individual sociopolitical and economic position, wealth, family safety and position, and a role of importance. The likely concerns in each of these areas are described along with actions that the ROK could take to moderate or overcome these concerns, as well as some options for communicating these actions to North Korean elites. More specific approaches to meeting elite needs are described for two kinds of individuals: North Korean People's Army (NKPA) generals and North Korean physicians.[1] The generals were chosen because of the implications for security problems if they rebel against unification; the physicians were chosen because they represent a class of elites essential to postunification conditions in North Korean society (medical care) who will not be allowed to perform their role under current anticipated ROK rules because they lack the training required for being licensed in the ROK.

It is, of course, impossible to determine how Korean unification will actually occur. While peaceful transition is clearly the most desired option, unification could also occur as the result of conflict or a North Korean government collapse. But across these scenarios, a favorable outcome to unification would depend on convincing Northern elites that unification will be something they can live with—not something unacceptably bad. The recommendations contained herein apply across these scenarios. Moreover, these recommendations need to be implemented as soon as possible to give North Korean elites time to learn about the ROK government plans for them and to develop confidence in those plans.

---

[1]   It is normal to speak of the Korean People's Army, or KPA, when referring to the North Korean military forces. However, to be clear, this report refers to the North Korean People's Army, or NKPA.

# Acknowledgments

I appreciate the opportunity given to me by the Korea Foundation to examine this extremely important topic.

I also appreciate the insights and advice provided by a number of North Korean defectors. These individuals, mostly former North Korean elites, have provided invaluable insights into their perspectives and the perspectives of their former peers.

Finally, I am grateful for the insightful reviews provided by colleagues Scott W. Harold of the RAND Corporation and independent author John Cha.

# CHAPTER ONE

# Introduction

For the Republic of Korea (ROK, also known as South Korea), and especially for the administration of former ROK President Park Geun-hye, achieving Korean unification has been a major objective. President Park sought a peaceful unification achieved in three stages: (1) trust-building, (2) commonwealth (confederation), and (3) full unification.[1] Well before coming into office, President Park explained her trust-building approach in a major article in *Foreign Affairs*.[2] But despite her efforts, North Korea—and especially its leader, Kim Jong-un—have resisted her trust-building efforts and have instead turned to regular confrontation with the ROK. This North Korean reaction should not be surprising: Because the ROK significantly dominates North Korea by most measures of national power, it would almost certainly assume the dominant position in any peaceful unification. Such an outcome would be unacceptable to the North Korean regime. Indeed, the North Korean Worker's Party Charter continues to describe conquest of the ROK as the objective of North Korea,[3] conquest being about the only

---

[1]  Ministry of Unification, *Initiative for Korean Unification*, Seoul, October 2015, p. 25.

[2]  Park Geun-Hye, "A New Kind of Korea: Building Trust Between Seoul and Pyongyang," *Foreign Affairs,* September/October 2011.

[3]  The Korean Workers' Party (KWP) Charter declares:

> [T]he present task of the [KWP] is to ensure the complete victory of socialism in the Democratic People's Republic of Korea and the accomplishment of the revolutionary goals of national liberation and the people's democracy in the entire area of the country. . . . the capital of the Democratic Republic of Korea shall be Seoul . . .

means for North Korea to assume the dominant position in a unified Korea.

Clearly, a peaceful unification of Korea would be preferred. But it is clear that North Korean elites would not agree to this if they feel it would be disadvantageous for them. Thus, the key question of this report is: What could be done that might convince North Korean elites that unification would be good for them? This is not a question normally asked. Many people in the ROK believe that North Korean elites will be and should be disenfranchised by unification because of their crimes and their exploitation of the North Korean people—and because North Korean elites, if allowed to retain their freedom in a unified Korea, may seek to sabotage the unification process. This is not a unique attitude: Similar concerns led the U.S. government to carry out the de-Ba'athification of the Iraqi government in the aftermath of 2003's Operation Iraqi Freedom,[4] and also to some U.S. actions against the Confederate South in the aftermath of the U.S. Civil War.[5]

This report postulates that a peaceful Korean unification is more likely if North Korean elites feel that unification will be good for them, or at least not unacceptably bad. It identifies conditions that North Korean elites would likely require to feel positive about unification. In the end, the South Korean government and people must decide whether to offer such conditions to North Korean elites; however, if they choose not to do so, by default they may have to pay a much higher price for unification.

---

According to Nicholas Eberstadt (*The End of North Korea,* Washington, D.C.: American Enterprise Institute Press, 1999), this is "a claim whose realization would require the prior removal of the ROK government."

[4]  The Iraqi Ba'ath Party was Saddam Hussein's party. To qualify for government service in Iraq under Saddam, most people were required to be Ba'ath Party members. After the United States conquered Iraq in 2003, it expelled a large number of party members from the Iraqi government, destabilizing that government and likely contributing to the insurgency that followed. See, for example, Miranda Sissons and Abdulrazzaq Al-Saiedi, "Iraq's de-Baathification Still Haunts the Country," *Al Jazeera,* March 12, 2013.

[5]  Dennis P. Halpin, "Korea and America, North and South," *NKNews,* March 23, 2015.

## Who Are North Korea's Elites?

Within any society, elite status implies a degree of position and empowerment. Historically, North Korea has used a political caste system, referred to as *songbun*, to classify its population. All adult North Koreans are divided into one of three groups, castes, or classes: core, wavering, and hostile. These three groups are then further divided into a total of 51 subgroups. Each individual's caste assignment is based on the regime's perception of the individual's political reliability, which is primarily measured relative to the historical loyalty to the regime of that person's family. Despite individual performance, there is relatively little upward mobility within the *songbun* system, but significant potential for downward mobility.[6]

The core class constitutes the baseline for North Korean elites. It is believed that perhaps 25 percent of the North Korean population fits within the core class.[7] There are roughly 17.7 million North Koreans over the age of 16, according to the North Korean 2008 census;[8] thus, some 4.4 million adults are likely members of the core class, well more than the total population of Pyongyang (estimated as between 2 million and 2.5 million),[9] where many of the true elites live. Moreover, many of the Pyongyang residents are lower- and midlevel officials who have only marginal influence on the fate of North Korea, and they may not most accurately be classed as elites. Based on discussions with North Korean defectors who have served in senior elite positions,[10] the number of senior elite personnel who would likely have major influ-

---

[6] Robert Collins, *Marked for Life: Songbun, North Korea's Social Classification System*, Washington, D.C.: The Committee for Human Rights in North Korea, June 6, 2012.

[7] Collins, 2012, p. iii.

[8] "DPR Korea 2008 Population Census: National Report," Pyongyang, DPR Korea: Central Bureau of Statistics, 2009.

[9] Several counties were removed from Pyongyang in 2010, lowering the population of the capital (see "Pyongyang Now More Than One-Third Smaller; Food Shortage Issues Suspected," *Asahi Shimbun*, July 17, 2010).

[10] I use the term *North Korean defectors* throughout for consistency and because this is the typical term used in the community. But I prefer the term *North Korean refugees*, as I feel that there should be no negative connotation for leaving North Korea.

ence on the future of North Korea is much smaller than the population of Pyongyang—perhaps numbering only several hundred thousand.[11] These individuals are the focus of this study.

## Methodology

This project involves trying to understand what would be needed to convince North Korean elites that unification would be good for them. It starts from basic human psychology: North Korean elites are not likely to be willing to agree to a peaceful unification unless they perceive it as either in their interests or at least not completely antithetical to their interests. It then proceeds to two kinds of initial sources for characterizing North Korean thinking: (1) what the North Korean regime is saying to convince elites that unification will be bad for them, and (2) media and other coverage of North Korean elite attitudes and the feelings of elites from other countries who have gone through changes in their government.[12] From these sources, I began by postulating the conditions that I believed would make North Korean elites comfortable with Korean unification.[13] In part, these conditions were derived from a document I wrote several years ago about how to deal with potential North Korean government collapse;[14] in writing it, I talked with approximately half a dozen North Korean elite defectors. Since writing that document, I received a large amount of input from South Koreans suggesting that they thought the policies I described would be needed to satisfy people in the Korean culture. Thus, many South Koreans, when these issues are explained to them, realize that there is a significant disconnect between the conditions that would

---

[11] The truly senior elites might number only 5,000 to 10,000. Discussions with North Korean defectors who served in senior elite positions, April–October 2016.

[12] I examined the German unification and the U.S. actions in Iraq after the 2003 invasion.

[13] Note that I rejected the concept of North Korean conquest of South Korea as a means of achieving unification, since it would not be peaceful.

[14] Bruce W. Bennett, *Preparing for the Possibility of a North Korean Collapse*, Santa Monica, Calif.: RAND Corporation, RR-331-SRF, 2013, pp. 103–138.

result from current ROK policy and what North Korean elites will feel that they need at unification. To better characterize the needed conditions, I selected two types of senior elite personnel and assessed their likely interests: North Korean People's Army (NKPA) generals and North Korean physicians. The generals were chosen because of the implications for security problems if they rebel against unification; the physicians were chosen because they represent a class of elites essential to postunification conditions in North Korean society (medical care) who will not be allowed to perform their role under current anticipated ROK rules because they lack the training required for being licensed in the ROK. I described the conditions of these two kinds of individuals today and then postulated their likely worries about unification. How would they feel about being punished for their behavior before unification, losing their positions, and so forth? What policies would be needed to gain their cooperation, and what policies would be totally unacceptable to these individuals? How should these policies be communicated to such North Korean elites? And what are the implications of not co-opting these individuals?

These efforts led to four policies/conditions for co-opting North Korean elites. I then began discussions with North Korean defectors who had served in elite positions to test and improve my understanding of these presumptions and necessary conditions for reducing North Korean elite resistance to unification.[15] These interviewees were once people of position and importance in North Korea who subsequently defected to South Korea. Since defecting, they have generally been unhappy about having lost their positions and importance. Many former senior elites provided important insights into what their peers would likely want in order to feel that unification is good for them. Through engaging in this process, I arrived at the need for a fifth condition (purpose), which I added after many discussions and deliberations. The discussions also provided a very different perspective on the entire unification process: These former North Korean elites feel that a regime collapse is fairly likely in the coming years, but do not feel that

---

[15] I interviewed about a dozen North Korean elite defectors. These individuals were drawn from the university, scientific, diplomatic, security, military, and merchant communities.

a North Korean government collapse is very likely (see Chapter Four). Many are also entrepreneurs prepared to adjust to a market society like South Korea.

## Report Outline

This report consists of four chapters. Chapter Two addresses the conditions that North Korean elites would likely seek to feel that unification would be good for them. It also discusses the policies that would need to be set in South Korea to achieve the desired outcomes and how those policies should be communicated to North Korean elites. Chapter Three applies these conditions to two kinds of elites: NKPA generals and North Korean physicians. It proposes specific actions that would be appropriate to meet some of their specific interests. Chapter Four examines a variety of scenarios that could lead to unification. It explains why the actions outlined in Chapters Two and Three would be relevant across the scenarios and therefore should be taken as soon as possible in preparation for however unification occurs.

# CHAPTER TWO

# What Will North Korean Elites Likely Want?

North Korean elites, and especially senior elites, are very privileged people in a repressive, draconian state. The elites enjoy their privileges, but they have also learned that activities to make money will generally give them a better life. Being privileged, however, does not give them the kind of safety and security one would expect in the United States or the ROK because of the brutal and somewhat arbitrary manner in which Kim Jong-un imposes his control over North Korean society.

Recognizing the nature of North Korean elite society, this chapter describes what North Korean elites would likely want in order to feel that Korean unification would be good for them. Initially, I identified four objectives for North Korean elites: individual safety and security, individual position, wealth, and family safety and position. After many discussions with senior North Korean defectors, I concluded that the elites would also want to have a role of importance—a way for them to contribute to Korean society and reestablish or continue to have a measure of influence. This chapter addresses the policies that South Korea needs to put in place to give North Korean elites a favorable impression of unification and how these policies could be communicated to North Korean elites.

Note that, as the ROK government formulates what it will offer North Korean elites, it must consider two things: what it will be prepared to offer well before unification to induce North Korean elites into thinking favorably about unification, and what it will actually offer at the time of unification. Well before unification, the ROK needs to create a positive image for the effect of unification on North Korean elites,[1] or those elites will likely resist any movement toward unification. As the transition to the actual unification occurs, favorable policies would also need to be in place to attract North Korean elites into agreeing to a peaceful unification. But if unification comes about as the result of conflict won by the ROK and the United States, some in the ROK government might feel that they need not be as generous because the North Koreans would then only have a choice between accepting what the ROK is prepared to offer or assuming a less-attractive life as a rebel or insurgent. In practice, however, the ROK government will likely want to avoid facing a serious North Korean insurgency in the aftermath of conflict that could impede the unified Korea's recovery, in the way that the insurgency in Iraq that started in 2003 impeded Iraqi recovery for many years. Ultimately, the ROK government must decide what it is prepared to offer and must balance generosity to North Korean elites to buy their favor and avoid their resistance with the cost of that generosity and the potential backlash that would be suffered in the ROK and among the lower classes in North Korea, at least some of whom will feel that North Korean elites were oppressors.

## Conditions in North Korea

Kim Jong-un's North Korea is a state with a small and ineffective planned economy, which is increasingly dominated by entrepreneurs and markets that operate outside of it, often illegally. Merchants and other entrepreneurs are able to stay in business by using bribery, and North Korean security officials (who are part of the elite) generally accept such bribery as a normal part of business while meeting their needs for daily life and, where possible, allowing them to enjoy a life of more than just survival.

---

[1]   North Korean elites may not retain quite the position or wealth after unification that they had before (although the losses they suffer in these areas should not be too serious), but their prospects for entrepreneurial activities should certainly be better and less risky after unification, and their safety and security should be far better, compared with being subject to Kim Jong-un's purges. This balance is important.

## Why Are the Expectations of the Senior Elites an Issue?

North Korean propaganda indoctrinates its elites to believe that unification, especially unification led by the ROK, would be a disaster for them. At unification, according to one North Korean propaganda statement, the United States and the ROK will "exterminate the core class families first."[2] Even if the broader ranks of the core class (the estimated 4.4 million adult elites) discount such regime statements as extreme and exaggerated, senior elites (perhaps several hundred thousand) likely will worry about their postunification fates. More broadly, North Korean elites—the core class—expect that unification led by the ROK would jeopardize their positions, safety, and security, potentially leading to their imprisonment or worse. These changes would affect not only the elites but also their families, giving them little potential for a good life, let alone the kind of privileged lives to which they have grown accustomed.[3]

If North Korean elites expect that unification will be bad for them and their families, they are unlikely to support it, potentially aborting the unification process either before it is formally declared or after; as a consequence, unification could fail. Indeed, many North Korean elites may well fight to the death against what they view has an unfavorable unification, much as Iraqis rebelled in the aftermath of the U.S. de-Ba'athification of Iraq in 2003 and beyond.

## What Would North Korean Elites Want from Korean Unification?

This section describes the five conditions that would likely help North Korean elites feel that unification could be good for them.

---

[2] Choi Song Min, "'Core' Class Urged to Pull the 'Wavering' into Line," *DailyNK*, March 23, 2016.

[3] In contrast, many East Germans looked forward to German unification, anticipating that they would have better lives.

### Individual Safety and Security

Having enjoyed privileged positions in North Korea, North Korean elites want to have their individual safety and security ensured (which they do not necessarily have now in North Korea) or at least not placed in serious jeopardy. Many worry that South Korea will treat them brutally, throwing them in prison, executing them, or perhaps simply allowing them to starve on the streets.[4] The ROK needs to consider a transitional justice system that minimizes the number of the elites, and especially senior elites, subject to criminal action. Justice should still be applied to North Koreans responsible for serious crimes, but some form of amnesty (full or partial) probably needs to be extended to others, or it will be difficult to imagine how resistance from North Korean elites can be minimized.

North Korean elites need only look at the example that South Korea has set with some of its former presidents. Former ROK Presidents Chun Doo-hwan (1980–1988) and Roh Tae-woo (1988–1993) were both tried and convicted on charges of of bribery and then treason, mutiny, and corruption. Former President Chun was sentenced to death, while President Roh received a 22½-year prison sentence (both were later pardoned). After he left office, President Roh Moo-hyun (2003–2008) committed suicide while under suspicion of bribery and corruption, and President Park Geun-hye has just had her impeachment confirmed.

Because of the inadequacies of the North Korean economy and the corruption in North Korean society, most North Korean elites have at least been active participants in the giving and taking of bribes;[5] can they expect any better treatment than the former ROK presidents received? At the same time, South Korea maintains a prison system with only about 50,000 spaces and has a criminal justice system con-

---

[4]  According to defector Kang Chol-hwan, "German unification completely deprived all East German Communist party and military leaders of their privileges and made them jobless." Without jobs, many could well face starvation. See Kang Chol-hwan, "Power Struggle Looms in N. Korea," *Chosun Ilbo*, May 8, 2009.

[5]  Bribery is the modus operandi of business in North Korea, considered to be business as usual and not a corrupt practice.

sistent with that number of incarcerated people.[6] It could take many years, and perhaps decades, to deal with all North Korean elites accused of crimes, with no way of confining so many potential criminals until their cases could be heard. Unless the ROK wants to vastly increase the size of its criminal justice and penal systems, it will need to offer amnesty to many North Koreans. This would be particularly true for most North Korean government officials; dismissing them from their positions and keeping them accused of crimes would leave North Korea without an effective government (see the discussion on positions below), although it is unlikely that North Korea would ever agree to such a ROK-led unification.

Thus, the only option for dealing with the realities of transitional justice most likely would be to provide selective but relatively broad amnesty for most North Koreans, and especially elites. This amnesty should not be extended to those accused of serious human rights violations, but likely should be applied to those accused of bribery and other financial law violations that have been required to conduct market activities and survive in North Korea.

The South Korean government needs to develop an approach to selective amnesty that considers at least (1) the probable patterns of illegal behavior among North Korean elites; (2) where to draw the lines of amnesty consistent with winning adequate support for unification among North Korean elites, while not losing the support of ordinary North Koreans and South Korean voters; (3) the capacity of the South Korean criminal justice system (both prison spaces and judicial capacity); and (4) the personnel requirements for sustaining a functioning government that can administer the territory of North Korea. Because ROK prison and judicial capacity are already consumed by ROK criminals, the ROK should be expanding its capacity in both areas, with particular attention being paid to the ability to respond to a sudden unification (and thus identifying capacities that could be mobilized in an emergency). But the South Korean government should also make its amnesty plans, expecting opposition to unification from any North

---

[6]  Bennett, 2013, pp. 123–125.

Korean elites who anticipate that unification will mean their imprisonment or worse.

An amnesty plan will not be popular among some in both South and North Korea. Some in South Korea will be angry at North Korean elites whom they believe exploited the broader North Korean population, especially knowing that they did so by breaking South Korean laws.[7] Many North Koreans will similarly be angry at the pardoning of their country's elites, whom they consider their exploiters. The ROK government should establish a panel in the near future with representatives from the ROK legal community and North Korean defectors familiar with application of the law in North and South Korea to propose basic approaches to transitional justice and appropriate adjustments required to the ROK penal system so that the unified Korean government can be prepared to apply the proposed transitional justice.[8] The panel should presumably support a substantial amnesty in recognition of the capacity of the ROK penal system, even if expanded. The panel should then publicly explain the need for selective amnesty to both the South and North Korean people and the nature of the crimes that will not be covered by that amnesty (in part to persuade North Koreans not to commit those crimes). This should be done now in the hope that some of the anger felt toward amnesty would dissipate over time before unification.

### Individual Position

North Korean elites, and especially senior elites, have been important and influential people. Their positions have given them favorable treatment in most aspects of life—they perceived this privilege as a means to contribute to the betterment of their country (this relates to elites' desire for a cause to which they contribute, giving them a sense of purpose and a feeling of personal efficacy). North Korean defectors inter-

---

[7]   Current ROK concepts of unification often assume that, after unification, ROK laws will become Korean laws applied to all of Korea and to the North retroactively. If unification happens under such ROK leadership, much of transitional justice would assess North Korean behavior relative to established ROK laws.

[8]   My colleague John Cha proposed this approach.

viewed for this report appear to feel a real loss as a result of not holding such positions in South Korean society.

The North Korean regime fully understands the importance of position to its elites. As defector Kang Chol-whan has noted,

> Kim Jong-il had the plight of former East German leaders photo-graphed and shown to North Korean cadres. And many members of the elite, though they detested Kim Jong-il, thought they had no alternative but to follow him for fear of losing their privileges if the regime collapsed.[9]

Fear of the loss of privilege, status, and personal motivation to live are among the reasons why it is hard for many North Korean elites to defect to South Korea. Still, elites do defect on occasion—some after encountering trouble in North Korea, others upon becoming disillu-sioned by the regime.

The United States set a bad precedent in this regard. After it defeated and occupied Iraq in 2003, the United States eliminated the Ba'ath party, removing members from their government jobs and con-fiscating some of their wealth. Today, there is broad consensus in the U.S. national security community that the across-the-board removal of Ba'ath party members from the Iraqi government was a major mis-take, contributing significantly to the subsequent inability to govern in Iraq and to the insurgency that raged for years after the invasion. But the U.S. failure to acknowledge this error and ROK's silence on whether they would take similar measures makes North Korean elites expect that they would suffer a similar fate in the event of unifica-tion in Korea, making unification a disaster for them and incentivizing them to resist it or seek to flee to other countries. Current ROK govern-ment policy reinforces this negative idea—its Committee for the Five Northern Korean Provinces designates ROK governors, mayors, and other officials to replace North Korean officials as part of Korean uni-fication under the auspices of the ROK.[10] And if North Korean elites

[9]  Kang, 2009.

[10] Alastair Gale and Kwanwoo Jun, "South Korea's Governors of Northern Provinces Don't—And Never Will—Govern," *Wall Street Journal*, March 17, 2014.

were replaced, they would likely be so stigmatized that they would have little ability to find any new job, let alone an attractive one.

The South Korean government should consider assuring North Korean elites that many of them would indeed be able to retain positions of significance during and after unification. Most importantly, the South Korean government should renounce plans for a broad decommunization of the North Korean government and instead plan to pursue a peaceful unification of the North and South Korean governments—with significant North Korean government personnel continuity, as opposed to a South Korean absorption of North Korea that would replace many North Korean authorities with ROK personnel.[11] This alteration of approach would be particularly important in reassuring North Korean technocrats; North Korean government functions would be seriously impaired if their services were lost.

The ROK could reinforce its efforts to unify Korea (as opposed to absorbing the North) if significant numbers of North Korean elite defectors were brought into the Committee for the Five Northern Korean Provinces. Moreover, the committee would appear more supportive if the roles designated in it were, for example, deputy governors or deputy mayors responsible for monitoring the unified government to avoid sabotage by retained North Korean elites who would still hold the roles of governors or mayors. North Korean officials are very familiar with political monitoring by state security authorities, so this kind of monitoring should not be surprising or unacceptable to them.

### Wealth

Until a famine in the mid-1990s, food and other consumables in North Korea generally came from the public distribution system. Such luxury items as televisions, refrigerators, or cars were usually gifts from the North Korean leader in recognition of particular loyalty and/or accomplishment. As the famine continued for several years, people experimented with illegal market activities to survive. Some merchants earned enough money not only to survive but to have a better life.

---

[11] This would require adjustments to the ROK Commission of the Five Northern Provinces, as discussed in Gale and Jun, 2014.

As elites in North Korea observed this development, many decided to become involved in similar market activities to give themselves the financial resources for better lives and to make them less dependent financially on the Kim family regime. In many cases, they were able to use their positions to the advantage of their market activities, especially in dealing with the security services.[12]

Ironically, many North Korean elites became entrepreneurs and capitalists. When observers comment on the appearance of wealth, shops, and restaurants in Pyongyang, they usually fail to recognize these developments have been the result of selective capitalism, rather than any success of the North Korean socialist economy. Some of the elites (especially in the security services) were also in positions where they could amass wealth by accepting bribes for allowing market activities to continue.

Like most people with wealth, North Korean elites will resist being forced to surrender that wealth and its associated favorable lifestyle as part of unification. Moreover, it may be difficult for the South Korean authorities to fully identify the wealth of many North Korean individuals because elites are already adept at hiding their wealth to avoid confiscation efforts by the regime and/or the security services. Some of the senior elites have been placing significant amounts in foreign currency and/or in overseas bank accounts in countries where they perceive their money to be relatively safe.[13] This lesson was driven home by the 2009 currency revaluation, which limited the amount of old North Korean currency that could be exchanged for new, allowing the North Korean government to seize the wealth of those who were poorly prepared. While elites might accept a modest level of tax applied to their observable wealth, more-aggressive measures would probably incite some level of resistance.

---

[12] Discussions with North Korean defectors who served in senior elite positions, April–October 2016.

[13] Discussions with North Korean defectors who served in senior elite positions, April–October 2016.

### Family Safety and Position

The North Korean political caste (*songbun*) system is designed to give privileges to the families of the elites. These privileges are important to the elites in part because families are extremely important in Korean culture. For example, the children of senior elites can be expected to be among those eligible to attend college—especially the more prestigious colleges within North Korea. Good political lineage within a family is often a prerequisite of college attendance, party membership, and jobs, especially for the better positions (although the individual's academic and professional performance are often important, as well).[14]

North Korean elites will likely fear losing this family preference at the time of unification. In practice, such free societies as South Korea may base opportunities for family members in part on family wealth but much less on family position, with more emphasis on individual performance. Thus, this issue for North Korean elites will be more difficult to make favorable. Still, allowing families to retain accumulated wealth and job positions will provide a degree of status for elites.

Meanwhile, there is an important advantage for families of elites in moving away from the North Korean system. In North Korea, if a senior elite family head is purged from his position and executed or imprisoned, it is fairly likely that the family of that individual will also be executed or imprisoned under the Kim family system. Guilt (political disloyalty) is attributed not just to the individual accused of disloyalty to the regime, but also to three generations of that individual's family.[15] Thus, when communicating with North Korean elites, it will be important to note that criminal justice in South Korea applies only to the individual and not to his or her family members, unless they have also been active participants in some crime.

---

[14] Kim Yoo-sung, "Who Goes to North Korea's Top Universities?" *NKNews*, August 26, 2015.

[15] "A 'wrongdoer' is often imprisoned with his/her parents and children. Kim Il-sung laid down the law in 1972: '[E]nemies of class, whoever they are, their seed must be eliminated through three generations.'" Blaine Harden, *Escape from Camp 14*, New York: Penguin Group, 2012, p. 6.

## Doing Something Important

A large number of nongovernmental defector organizations have been created by North Korean defectors seeking to bring about change in their former home through a variety of activities. These include radio broadcasts into the North, balloons sent into North Korea carrying leaflets, DVDs and USB drives with movies and television shows, and other messages. The defectors are attempting to do something important despite no longer having a position that allows them to directly affect change. As a result, a large number of nongovernmental defector organizations have been created in South Korea to bring about change in North Korea. The feelings among these individuals are very intense: For them, bringing about change gives meaning and importance to their lives.

Given this shared attitude across the elite defectors with whom I had contact, I am convinced that many North Korean elites will have a similar desire during and after unification. Allowing North Korean elites to retain their government positions or otherwise obtain positions of importance will give them the opportunity to do something meaningful. Alternatively, allowing elites to take on humanitarian roles within North Korea would also provide such an opportunity. This consideration should be taken into account when planning for Korean unification; it would allow North Koreans—especially North Korean elites—to organize themselves in ways to help their fellow citizens adapt during the unification process.

## The Likely Anxieties Among North Korean Elites

The key issue is how to help North Korean elites feel that unification will be good for them. Such a judgment will undoubtedly be relative to their perception of their life today under the rule of Kim Jong-un.[16] Across the five conditions described in this chapter, how do North

---

[16] They may also consider how their life would change if they decide to resist unification, although a decision to resist would potentially be made in anger rather than based on calculated logic.

Korean elites likely feel now, and what do they likely believe about how their lives would change after unification? We do not know for sure, as we have no real access to those individuals. But some information does leak out, and North Korean defectors also provide insights.

Based on discussions with North Korean elite defectors and media descriptions of elite lives in North Korea,[17] it appears possible that many senior elites feel that they would be worse off after unification than they are today, given their current expectations of what would happen at unification. The North Korean regime has made every effort to indoctrinate elites into believing that unification would be disastrous for them. This perspective results in part from the regime's declarations about the likely extermination of core class families upon unification and also from the experiences of East German elites upon German unification. Unfortunately, this view may be sustained by the experiences of North Korean defectors because many find life in South Korea to be difficult. These messages get back into North Korea through both direct communications and regime attempts to demonstrate the bad effects of defection. Especially damaging are individuals who redefect to North Korea.[18]

However, North Korean elites' levels of anxiety about unification would likely decline if the ROK were to adopt friendlier unification policies. North Korean elites would undoubtedly harbor uncertainties about whether they could trust the ROK government and thus would maintain some level of concern, but the most serious anxieties could be reduced. This would be particularly true for the many North Korean elites who have become entrepreneurs. They may well feel that unification has the potential for placing them in a better position for economic success, although they would also face many uncertainties that would put such success at risk.

---

[17] The ROK media carries many stories about life in North Korea; the *DailyNK* is a particularly valuable online resource. Another valuable resource is *NKNews*, which carries a regular column written by North Korean defectors.

[18] Greg Scarlatoiu, Jana Johnson, and Miran Song, "Re-Defection to North Korea: Exaggeration or the Beginning of a Trend?" *NKNews*, January 24, 2013.

## Putting Needed Policies in Place

South Korea cannot wait until the verge of action to start sharing information about revised unification plans and how North Korean elites could expect to be treated. Immediately prior to unification, during a crisis, or at the outset of a conflict, North Korean elites would be highly unlikely to trust statements by South Korea, fearing that these statements would be intended merely to dupe them into an unfavorable unification. Instead, policies and plans that North Korean elites would find favorable need to be developed in South Korea in the near future so they have time to achieve a measure of credibility with their intended audiences. The South Korean government would also need to pass laws associated with the unification process and begin amassing the funds required, thereby demonstrating that South Korean intentions are sincere and have substance. These policies and plans need to be communicated into North Korea promptly, regularly, and consistently to convince North Korean elites that South Korea really has taken an approach to unification that will be more acceptable and includes a place for them in a unified Korea.

### Developing New Policies

This chapter touched on key policies that the South Korean government needs to consider implementing so that North Korean elites can feel that unification could be good for them. These can be summarized as follows:

- **Policies on transitional justice.** South Korea needs some combination of a substantial but selective amnesty program for North Koreans and a substantial expansion of its prison and judicial capacities. Many South and North Koreans may oppose amnesty for crimes other than limited bribery, but South Koreans are also likely to resist paying for greater prison and judicial capacities. Options and trade-offs should be discussed in South Korea and at least some decisions made regarding incentives to encourage better behavior by North Korean elites (and others) and to help all involved prepare for unification should sudden political change develop in North Korea in the coming years.

- **Policies on government and other positions and Workers' Party of Korea's status.** At the very least, the ROK does not want to dismiss North Korean government employees who have the institutional memory and skills needed to keep government in North Korea working. In addition, the ROK must recognize that any North Korean leader dismissed from a government position could well assume a leadership position among the anti-unification forces in North Korea. Would the ROK be better off retaining that government employee (where he or she might be unreliable) or potentially having to fight them and others who might organize a resistance? South Korea also needs to decide what to do about North Korean elites who are professionals because, in many cases, those professionals will not meet South Korean standards. This will be particularly true with such positions as physicians and engineers. Rather than exclude these professionals from continuing their practices and thus denying whole categories of services in much of North Korea, the South Korean government needs to develop remedial training programs for these professionals while keeping them employed to some extent.

- **Policies on the wealth of North Koreans.** Some North Koreans apparently have wealth because they have acted like entrepreneurs in recent years or because they have taken bribes and/or defrauded the government. At least some of this wealth is hidden in overseas bank accounts that may be difficult to find. The ROK needs to decide how to handle this money, recognizing that non-elite North Koreans may feel that this wealth is ill-gotten gains, while the wealthy may be driven to rebellion if too much of it is taken from them. Full disclosure of this wealth and a modest tax applied to it may be the best approach.

- **Policies on the families of elites.** Many countries provide advantages to the families of high-ranking officials and wealthy individuals. North Korea goes to an extreme with its political caste system. A unified Korea will not match the relative family benefits in North Korea today: The difference between North Korean elites and nonelites today is likely greater than will exist after unification. But neither should the unified Korea punish family members of North Korean elites for the crimes of their kin. South Korea should be very clear that, after unification, it will not apply the North Korean rule that three generations of the family would punished for a family member's crimes.[19] In practice, the unified Korea would naturally provide some form of family benefits, especially to North Korean officials who have retained their positions and/or have accumulated significant wealth. Senior North Korean elites anxious to maintain advantages for their families would likely be best served by accumulating wealth in the period before unification.

- **Policies on providing opportunities for elites to contribute to a broader social cause post-unification.** After unification, all Koreans should be encouraged to work for the benefit of their country and its people. North Korean government officials should be allowed to continue working for the unified Korean government—giving those officials a continuing sense of individual purpose—unless they are responsible for serious crimes that would not allow for amnesty. In addition, South Korea should review its laws and rules for licensing such professionals as physicians, engineers, and contractors, and, where possible, allow North Koreans in these professions to continue working, while providing advanced training to allow for eventual full licensure.[20]

### Communicating These Policies

It will take considerable time to convince North Korean elites that the policies described have actually been adopted in sincerity, will be implemented after unification, and that South Korea holds no malice toward them unless they have committed serious crimes. Thus, the South Korean government needs to promptly decide which North Korean elite–favorable policies it will implement and then begin the

---

[19] This characteristic of North Korea was noted previously.

[20] See Chapter Three for specific recommendations on how North Korean physicians, as an example of professionals, ought to be handled.

process of communicating these policies to North Korea. The ROK should take advantage of every opportunity for this communication:

- South Korea should organize and support extensive radio broadcasts into North Korea that describe unification plans, especially the policies outlined above. These broadcasts should be done regularly and comprehensively, so that the vast majority of North Koreans hear about these policies and, over time, start to believe them. These broadcasts should be done not just on defector radio stations but also on ROK government stations.[21] Defector groups operating radio stations for broadcast into North Korea should receive subsidies from the ROK government to help them serve as an alternative source of assurance for North Korean elites.

- South Korea should organize and support efforts to send leaflets into North Korea that describe the policies outlined above. The North Korean regime will be very angry at these leaflets. To make these efforts politically acceptable in South Korea, North Korea should be warned that if it carries out provocations against South Korea (e.g., missile or nuclear weapon tests), leafleting North Korea could be a ROK response. Since North Korea can be expected to commit provocations, this approach would give justification to what might otherwise be viewed by some South Koreans as provocation against the North. Moreover, threatening such a response beforehand, especially once North Korea recognizes that the ROK is serious, may also have the effect of deterring some North Korean provocations.

---

[21] This proposal will be controversial. Some in the ROK will worry that such aggressive broadcasts will sour relations between North and South Korea, while others will think that broadcasts are ineffective because of North Korean information-control procedures. However, at least one survey suggests that more than 10 percent of North Korean defectors polled in South Korea had listened to outside radio broadcasts before leaving the North. Of course, it is expected that North Korean defectors would have listened to outside radio broadcasts more than the average person in North Korea, but as the report on this poll suggests, if the actual number of people in North Korea who listen to outside broadcast is only 1 percent, that would still be several hundred thousand people—not a small number. See Young Howard, "North Korean Audience for Open Radio for North Korea," *DailyNK*, February 5, 2006.

- South Korea and the United States should make every effort to reach North Korean overseas workers and provide them with information on the policies and plans for unification. Many of these workers are from elite families. If they become convinced of the information they are provided, they will carry those messages home to their families—which will likely include their extended families—thus, reaching exactly the audience that this information needs to reach.[22]
- The South Korean Ministry of Unification should make a series of fictional movies in which the story line shows North Korean elite families going through the process of unification. These movies would help the people of South Korea better understand why some of the compromises described herein are required to achieve peaceful unification. The movies will also help people in North Korea understand the South Korean unification policies and begin to believe in them. If done well, such movies would likely become extraordinarily popular in North Korea and would likely reach many North Korean elites.

Other methods of communicating the policies for unification should also be used where possible—these are but examples.

---

[22] This approach was recommended by a senior elite North Korean defector during an interview, September 2016.

# CHAPTER THREE

# North Korean People's Army Generals and North Korean Physicians

To clarify the issues faced in creating a positive image of unification in the minds of North Korean elites, this chapter focuses on two specific kinds of elite personnel in North Korea: a notional NKPA general and a hypothetical North Korean physician.[1] Both would be members of the core class within the North Korean political caste system. Both pose a risk to a combined Korean government because either would have the potential to organize and/or participate in a resistance movement. And both, but especially physicians, could play important roles in the North Korean population perceiving that safety and security have been achieved in a unified Korea.

This chapter describes the efforts that would likely be required to convince NKPA generals and North Korean physicians that unification would be good for them. It does so by initially describing the current conditions for these two kinds of individuals, and then proposing the policies and programs that should be put in place to give them a positive view of unification.

---

[1] As noted in Chapter One, the generals were chosen because of the implications for security problems if they rebel against unification. The physicians were chosen because they represent a class of elites essential to postunification conditions in North Korean society (medical care) but who will not be allowed to perform their role under current anticipated ROK rules because they lack the training required for ROK licensing.

## Their Current Conditions

This section describes some general characteristics of NKPA generals and North Korean physicians. It addresses both the overall nature of the individuals in these categories and the potential threats they would pose if dissatisfied with their circumstances in unification.

### NKPA Generals

The NKPA has approximately 1.2 million total active-duty personnel.[2] Of these, generals make up approximately 0.1 percent, or roughly 1,200 personnel.[3] Simply from these numbers, it should be clear that the position of a NKPA general is very high in the North Korean hierarchy. Of necessity, such an individual would be a member of the Korean Worker's Party and part of the core class.

If the NKPA generals see little prospect of a future for themselves and their families after unification, they could become a major source of resistance to unification. Some would likely become major leaders in any insurgency that develops. Generals who think that unification will hurt them may also be able to abort the unification process by taking military action against the ROK before their military units are dissolved. And even if the North Korean military forces are disarmed and demobilized, there appear to be many places in North Korea where arms are stored, including thousands of underground facilities.[4]

---

[2]  ROK Ministry of National Defense, *2014 Defense White Paper*, January 6, 2015, p. 261.

[3]  North Korea identifies generals as starting at the rank of major general, similar to the Chinese system. Both have "senior colonels" who are the rough equivalent to U.S. military brigadier generals. "From December 1991 through the end of May 1995, promotions and assignments of nearly 800 general officers (many only in their 50s) were noted in the general officer corps of approximately 1,200" (*Korea North: Energy Policy, Laws and Regulation Handbook: Strategic Information and Developments,* Vol. 1 [Strategic Information and Developments], Washington, D.C.: International Business Publications, USA, March 3, 2008, p. 180). The number 1,200 may include senior colonels, although promotion discussions tend to exclude them. See, for example: Stephan Haggard, "Military Promotions in the DPRK," Peterson Institute of International Economics, August 13, 2013.

[4]  "A South Korean intelligence source estimates that there are several hundred large underground factories in North Korea and more than 10,000 smaller facilities. Joseph Bermudez, the author of three books on the North Korean military, puts the total number between

It would take many months, if not years, to secure all of these weapons. In the meantime, generals with the loyalty of many officers and soldiers—and potentially even civilians—could pose an insurgency threat against safety and security in North Korea, thereby endangering unification.

On the other hand, if the combined Korean government is able to co-opt these generals, they could assist with the safety and security needed in the unification process. They could play an important role in allowing their military forces to be disarmed and put to work in ways to improve the dilapidated infrastructure in North Korea.[5] They could have a positive influence on their former peers or subordinates who may be considering resisting unification, possibly convincing those individuals to terminate their defiance and accept unification. They could also help organize efforts to protect companies and communities from either insurgency or criminal activity. At least some of the NKPA generals are already entrepreneurs, and, with appropriate access to financial resources, could become leaders of small or even large businesses in the unified Korea.

### North Korean Physicians

According to several sources, the North Korean population of about 24 million people had roughly one physician for every 300 people in 2003,[6] or about 80,000 total physicians. By comparison, the ROK had about one physician for every 625 people in 2003,[7] and about one physician for every 470 people in 2012,[8] or about 107,000 total physicians in 2012. It is unclear why North Korea has a greater density of physicians, although the numbers may reflect the relative difficulty of get-

---

11,000 to 14,000" (Barbara Demick, "Vision on Tunnels Drives N. Korean Defense," *Los Angeles Times*, November 28, 2003).

[5]  Options for transitioning the North Korean military forces are described in more detail in Bennett, 2013, pp. 186–204.

[6]  See, for example, "Health > Physicians > Per 1,000 People: Countries Compared," Nationmaster.com, 2003.

[7]  "Health > Physicians > Per 1,000 People: Countries Compared," 2003.

[8]  Central Intelligence Agency, "Physicians Density," *World Factbook*, undated.

ting a medical degree in South Korea or the number of other health care professionals (such as physician's assistants) available there.

Based on discussions with North Korean defectors, it appears that most physicians in North Korea are considered only to be midlevel elites. Indeed, even doctors on the faculties of top medical schools are not considered senior-level elites.[9]

Medical conditions in North Korea are incredibly poor. According to one foreign doctor who worked in North Korea:

> In my role as an emergency doctor, I also visited a number of other medical institutions besides the ten hospitals and three orphanages to which I was assigned. In every locale, I witnessed horrific conditions. There were no bandages, no scalpels, no antibiotics, no operating rooms—only ramshackle wooden beds supporting starving children waiting to die. Doctors used empty beer bottles as vessels for intravenous dripping. Safety razors were used as scalpels. I even witnessed an appendectomy performed without anesthesia. Meanwhile I found out, through my own investigations, about government storehouses and diplomatic shops carrying large stocks of bandages and other medical supplies for privileged classes.[10]

According to a North Korean doctor who defected to South Korea, scarcity of medicines in North Korea forced doctors to go into the hills to collect herbs that were used in place of standard medicines. The doctors were often required to spend one month a year doing so.[11]

Because many North Korean physicians have little experience with modern medicine and equipment, those who leave North Korea for life in South Korea are not allowed to practice medicine; they lack the training needed to practice modern medicine consistent with South Korean standards. South Korea appears not to have developed enrich-

---

[9]  Interview with a North Korean defector whose father was a medicine professor in North Korea, August 2016.

[10]  Norbert Vollertsen, "A Depraved Society We Can't Ignore," *American Enterprise*, July/August 2005.

[11]  Barbara Demick, *Nothing to Envy*, New York: Spiegel and Grau, 2009, pp. 106–107.

ment training that could be used to prepare North Korean doctors for licensing, instead insisting that they start over again in medical school before starting medical practice.[12]

## Potential Reactions to Unification

Taking the five objectives discussed in Chapter Two, it seems clear that NKPA generals and North Korean physicians would fear the results of Korean unification. Many generals have likely been abusive to their soldiers and taken bribes (and/or skimmed unit funds),[13] and thus would likely fear imprisonment or execution in the aftermath of unification, both because of their offenses and because they pose a potential threat to the unified government. They may also fear subordinates seeking revenge because of their abusive behavior. And they would likely have high fears of losing their jobs/positions, privileges, influence, and even their wealth, expecting that they would be expelled from the military. These losses would severely affect their families.

In contrast, North Korean physicians would likely be most afraid of being expelled from their positions (medical service), given the pattern of North Korean physician defectors who have been denied approval to practice medicine in South Korea and forced to return to medical school or take another job. The loss of their jobs would also jeopardize their wealth and the privileges of their families.[14]

The issue of doing something important is more complicated. If North Korean physicians are not allowed to practice medicine after unification, as many of them likely expect, then they would not be able

---

[12] Demick, 2009.

[13] "However, discipline within the Korean People's Army is reportedly plummeting, with frequent desertions and thefts. This is because regular soldiers are bearing the brunt of corruption and embezzlement by senior officers, particularly with regards to food" (Kim Chae Hwan, "Morale of North Korean Soldiers Drops Despite Visit by Kim Jong Un," *DailyNK*, December 8, 2016).

[14] If they cannot work as physicians and are not thoroughly established as entrepreneurs, they are not going to maintain their lifestyle or anything close over time—a disaster for them.

to take on important responsibilities, as they are accustomed to. But the NKPA general may feel that if he were expelled from his military position, he could assume a significant role in the resistance against the unified Korean government, and that doing so would be helping the North Korean people. This, of course, is not an outcome that a unified Korean government would want.

## Specific Policies and Actions for Generals and Physicians

The policies and plans recommended in Chapter Two should provide a viable environment for both NKPA generals and North Korean physicians relative to their interest in safety and security and their concerns about maintaining their existing wealth. But the actions taken for both of these kinds of individuals are different relative to providing them positions, and thus providing for future wealth, taking care their families, and giving them an important purpose. This section addresses those issues of positions and purpose, although it also touches on how their families would be taken care of and their potential for continuing to maintain and accumulate wealth.

### NKPA Generals

At the time of German unification, "Bonn decided that all former NVA soldiers over 50 would be given early retirement."[15] These older personnel were required to leave the military within four months of unification. The West Germany–dominated combined government was unprepared to have former East German generals, colonels, and other senior personnel retained in the military in positions where they would be able to give orders to West German soldiers. A similar situation should be expected in Korea: Very few (if any) NKPA generals will be allowed to remain within the combined military, and those individuals will almost certainly be kept in advisory (e.g., policy) positions, rather than command positions.

---

[15]  Dale Herspring, *Requiem for an Army: The Demise of the East German Military*, Lanham, Md.: Rowman and Littlefield, 1998, pp. 150.

Figure 3.1 provides an overview of the recommended approach for dealing with NKPA generals. The fundamental question for those individuals will be whether it is time for them to retire. As was done with the East German military, it would be best to establish rules for the age at which North Korean military personnel would be required to retire, but also allow those personnel to continue with some form of professional activity past that time if they were capable of performing useful functions, as some almost certainly would be.

At what age should North Korean military retirement be set? That depends on the number of personnel at the different ages. The 2008 North Korean census is the only source on the age of North Korean military personnel that I was able to identify. But those estimates involve a clear falsification of the number of military personnel of age 30 and older. In attempting to correct this, I estimate that the number of North Korean military personnel (not just generals) is approximately 9,500 for ages 50–54, 4,300 for ages 55–59, 1,400 for ages 60–64, 300 for ages 65–69 (presumably mainly generals), and about 30 for age 70

**Figure 3.1**
**Transitioning NKPA Generals**

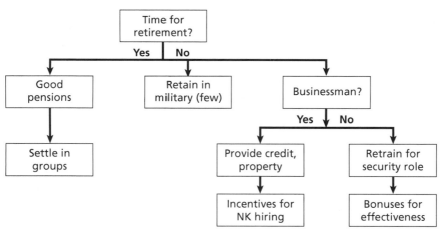

and older.[16] These numbers do not include North Korean security services personnel. From these numbers, it appears that Korea probably would not want to retire all military personnel over the age of 50—that would be too large a group. Instead, the age of 60 appears to be a more viable threshold for pressing most North Korean military personnel to retire.[17]

Many of these 1,700 or so senior personnel over the age of 60 could or should be offered retirement (or even forced into retirement), consistent with practices of the ROK and other military forces. They should be offered attractive pensions and medical benefits if they do retire. Part of the retirement benefits should include housing within communities of North Korean former senior officers, where the activities of these individuals can more easily be monitored to avert their participation in insurgency and/or criminal activities (with serious penalties threatened should these personnel become involved in such activities).[18]

---

[16] "DPR Korea 2008 Population Census: National Report," 2009. Table 1 of this report shows the total North Korean population by age and gender. Table 2 shows similar data by location, but accounts for some 702,000 fewer people (662,000 fewer men). Other authors note that this difference is apparently the North Korean accounting of their military population, which they wish not to locate geographically. The estimate of 702,000 is clearly too small for the North Korean military, and it is particularly errant in the numbers of military personnel ages 30 or older. I previously created a "corrected" estimate of the North Korean military population by age, including the numbers contained in this paragraph; this is a very rough estimate.

[17] The age of 60 is chosen in part because North Korean military personnel in their 50s are unlikely to want to retire. In addition, based on the estimates of this paragraph, there may be more than 15,000 North Korean personnel age 50 and older, but only 1,700 age 60 or older. If the retirees were offered a retirement payment of roughly one-half the salary of comparable ROK officers (I estimate that one-half would be about 50 million won per officer per year), the price of the retirement of everyone over age 50 would be nearly a trillion won per year, probably too large an amount to get broad support from the Korean population. Retiring those over 60 would lower the aggregate cost to about 100 billion won—still a large amount, but much less so.

[18] Locating North Korean general officer retirees in the same areas raises the risks that they could meet together often and plan actions against unified Korea. These risks could be moderated by settling some retired South Korean general officers in the same communities and asking them to monitor the behavior of their North Korean counterparts.

For generals under the age of 60 and those 60 and older who do not retire, a couple of different employment options should be offered. Some of these generals may already be businessmen, having been involved in the North Korean black market or other market activities. They may wish to continue in their roles as businessmen; their ability to succeed in business under the restrictive North Korean business environment suggests that they may be able to succeed in the more business-friendly environment likely to prevail after unification. Therefore, provisions should be made to provide these individuals with financial capital and property consistent with the size of business that they run. Because a major concern in North Korea postunification will be unemployment, it would be a mistake to lose whatever employment these North Korean generals would be capable of supporting. Indeed, it would be wise to offer them incentives for hiring more North Koreans to assist with the overall unemployment challenge. Many of the generals' former subordinates may wish to work for them in other capacities, having established relationships and faith in their leadership. But the generals' businesses will need to be subject to rules that would prevent them from becoming criminal activities and to inspections that would verify that no criminal activities are taking place.

Other North Korean generals may be more inclined to take employment involving security functions. The combined Korean government could connect them with ROK and other businesses seeking to establish themselves in North Korea. The generals could assist in the security function for these companies and would presumably have access to former subordinates who would also be looking for employment and would be anxious to perform such a role. As the United States has learned in Iraq, there are some significant differences between the training of military personnel for combat operations and the training of personnel for security operations. Thus, the ROK government would want to do some retraining of former North Korean military personnel to prepare them for security operations. Using North Koreans in these roles could be helpful because they would better know the terrain, facilities, and potential threats in North Korea. These security personnel should be offered bonuses for defeating security threats against the companies they are protecting. Nevertheless, the companies employing them would also want to monitor their activities for some time to make sure that they do not get involved in criminal activity that would jeopardize the companies.

## North Korean Physicians

If current ROK policy with North Korean defectors is followed, North Korean physicians would not be allowed to continue to serve in that capacity during and after unification. Doing so would be disastrous for medical care in North Korea. While the North Korean medical system is clearly broken, it appears to be due more to a lack of resources than poor physician care. With that in mind, the best solution for North Korean physicians would be to allow them to continue to practicing under certain constraints while trying to provide them advanced training toward full ROK medical licensure. The alternative option for providing health care in North Korea would be to move tens of thousands of ROK physicians immediately into North Korea, an approach that undoubtedly would not be feasible.[19] Still, South Korea should plan to move a few hundred ROK physicians into the North to serve as consultants, trainers, and monitors in support of a prompt improvement in medical care in North Korea.[20]

The proposed approach for North Korean physicians is shown in Figure 3.2. As soon as possible, the ROK should establish an advanced training program for North Korean physicians that would allow them to eventually become fully licensed doctors with the resources and under the laws of South Korea. That program could then be tested with the North Korean physicians who defect over the coming years to refine the program and make sure it is effective. When the program

---

[19] Moving a substantial number of South Korean physicians to North Korea would also reduce the supply of medical services in South Korea, likely causing significant increases in the cost of medical care in South Korea, an unwanted outcome.

[20] A few hundred ROK doctors moved to the North may not make enough difference. Based on the experience of Iraq, where Iraqis thought the all-powerful United States would solve all problems as soon as Saddam disappeared, there is a risk in making too small an effort to improve the lives of North Koreans postunification. It might be necessary to create a major improvement in health and sanitation (especially since diseases might flow south more readily in the wake of unification) to forestall a turn toward insurgency.

is fully applied after unification, some North Korean physicians will refuse to take the advanced training. But rather than prevent them from practicing medicine at all, they should be licensed under a category that allows them to continue practicing in North Korea (and only North Korea) with some significant limitations, including the drugs they are allowed to prescribe and medical procedures they are allowed to perform. This category of physician would only be allowed to continue with what they could have done in North Korea before unification.

Hopefully, most of the North Korean physicians will want to pursue advanced training,[21] which should be organized in segments. The completion of each segment would allow incrementally more-complete medical licensure. For example, a North Korean general practitioner would need to be trained on advanced antibiotics before being authorized to prescribe them. North Korean surgeons would be required to train on the basics of surgery as practiced in South Korea. These surgeons should also be given the opportunity to train for spe-

**Figure 3.2**
**Transitioning Physicians: Sustain the Availability of Medical Care in North Korea**

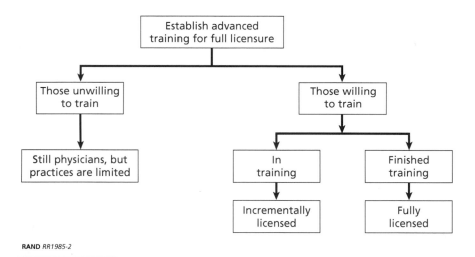

RAND RR1985-2

---

[21] While this training could also be called *remedial training*, such terminology would have a pejorative connotation that should be avoided.

cialty surgery, such as thoracic surgery or neurosurgery. These training programs should likely resemble standard training in such specialties, including a period of internship with fully trained South Korean specialists in these areas. In some cases, South Korean medical trainers could be sent to North Korea and rotate among communities with positions to provide the in-person training when necessary. In specialty areas, a cadre of South Korean physicians could be prepared to rotate into North Korea and take over from North Korean physicians while North Koreans spend time in South Korea doing their hands-on training. The bottom line is that the advanced training would be incremental, which is not all that different from advanced medical training in many countries today, except that the North Korean physicians would be starting from a much lower level of training.

# CHAPTER FOUR

# Planning Across Scenarios

This chapter examines the two types of scenarios that could lead to Korean unification (peaceful and via conflict) and argues that, in either case, successful unification will likely require that North Korean elites feel that unification will be good for them.[1] Because it will probably take many years to convince most North Korean elites of this perspective, this conclusion suggests that South Korea should work aggressively and with urgency to formulate a program associated with the efforts outlined in Chapters Two and Three; once put in place, the ROK should then implement its messaging campaign.

The unification of Korea is unlikely to be a single event. If it occurs as the result of war or the collapse of the North Korean government, simply securing the territory would likely take months—and perhaps years—if third parties like China intervene. Even without such intervention, securing the territory of North Korea will not be easy because a North Korean resistance movement can be expected in nonpeaceful scenarios. Such a resistance could take years to overcome; it could even prove impossible. Even if there is a peaceful unification with a formal start date, resistance still might arise, requiring anywhere from months to years for resolution. In short, it is entirely possible that unification might occur as the result of the disappearance of the North Korean

---

[1] Conceptually, Korean unification could also occur as the result of a North Korean conquest of South Korea, leading to a North Korean absorption of the South. As long as the U.S.–South Korean alliance remains strong, such an outcome seems very unlikely. It is therefore not considered herein.

regime, and yet not be complete because of continuing—and potentially substantial—organized resistance to the unification process.

## Unification as the Result of Conflict

Korean unification could result from a wide range of conflict scenarios. These include a North Korean invasion of South Korea (either successful or failed), an escalation spiral sparked by North Korean provocations, or even the collapse of the North Korean government. In any of these cases, unification would likely occur as the result of ROK and U.S. forces intervening to (1) seize North Korean territory, (2) replace the senior leadership of the North Korean regime, and (3) bring North Korea under ROK control. A North Korean invasion of South Korea or a North Korean provocation that escalates out of control would almost certainly involve considerable military conflict before ROK and U.S. forces were to enter North Korea, and conflict could even intensify once that occurred. A North Korean government collapse would likely involve conflict beginning with ROK and U.S. forces entering North Korea. Unless the North Korean military commanders perceived that unification by ROK absorption would be good for them, they would likely fight the intervening ROK and U.S. forces. And in all conflict cases, conflict would likely continue for a substantial period of time after a ROK and U.S. "victory," perhaps even years: Many North Korean forces that are not defeated and neutralized would be expected to transition to resistance operations and/or criminal activity, even if initially disarmed.

No one outside of North Korea wants to see a second Korean War. Even if conflict is limited to the intervention of ROK and U.S. forces in North Korea because of the collapse of the North Korean government, hundreds of thousands of South Koreans could lose their lives as a result of North Korean nuclear and/or other weapons of mass destruction or conventional attacks, unless North Korean military forces were co-opted by the ROK and the United States.[2] And, to reiterate a point made above, North Korean forces are unlikely to be co-opted if their commanders think that unification will be bad for them. As the recent North Korean defector Thae Yong-ho explained, "In order to have them betray Kim, the upper bracket of North Korea must believe that they will face no disadvantages in a unified Korea."[3] As noted at the beginning of Chapter Two, Thae's statement appears most applicable to peaceful unification, although, even in that scenario, North Korean elites may be prepared to accept some compromises. But today, well before unification, the ROK will gain little North Korean support for any kind of unification without a favorable depiction of the future for the elites. North Korean indoctrination is intended to prevent this perspective from developing, as described earlier.

Every effort made now to convince North Korean elites that unification will be good for them increases the probability of reducing the damage that could result from conflict in Korea leading to unification. The more that North Korean elites believe or even hope that unification will be good for them, the less they will want to hurt South Korean forces or impose damage on the South. Ideally, many North Korean senior military will agree to be co-opted and support the unification process. Of course, no matter what South Korea and the United States do, some North Korean elites will be unable to believe what is said about unification being good; they may thus be prepared to do substantial damage to ROK and U.S. interests. In the aftermath of a conflict, the ROK and United States should be prepared to sort out which North Korean elites are favorable to unification and which are not and to continue these efforts over some time. The ROK and the United States will then need to isolate and subdue former North Koreans who cause problems.

---

[2]   This kind of outcome could be avoided if ROK and U.S. forces were able to militarily neutralize all major North Korean threats promptly, but the size of the North Korean forces and the uncertainties surrounding the locations of North Korean weapons of mass destruction, missiles, artillery, and special operations forces make prompt neutralization very unlikely.

[3]   "N. Korea Purging Descendants of Anti-Japanese Guerrillas: Defector," *Korea Herald*, January 27, 2017.

Unfortunately, it seems unlikely that there are many North Korean elites today who think that a ROK-led unification will be good for them. It is therefore critical that the ROK begin as soon as possible to pursue efforts—such as those suggested in Chapters Two and Three— that North Korean elites will find convincing, since these will take time to reach their target audiences, sink in, and acquire credibility.

## Peaceful Unification

The ROK is very much focused on peaceful unification as the only alternative it wants to pursue. Peaceful unification would involve the leaders of the ROK and North Korea agreeing to take steps toward unification. At the strategic level, under the Park Geun-hye administration, the ROK defined those steps as involving trust-building, commonwealth (confederation), and full unification.[4] Kim Jong-un has clearly rebuffed this approach. In a January 1, 2017, speech, he said his people must "wage a dynamic pan-national struggle to thwart the moves of the traitorous and sycophantic anti-reunification forces like Park Geun Hye."[5] Since then-President Park was one of the strongest advocates of the ROK vision of peaceful unification, Kim was clearly suggesting that he has a very different view of unification, presumably one involving conquest of the ROK by North Korea.[6] The ROK concept of a peaceful unification thus appears infeasible as long as Kim Jong-un remains in power. Defector Thae Yong Ho has said that "Kim Jong Un's days are numbered," and he "vowed to help bring down the North Korean leader, calling that the only way to resolve the nuclear issue and unify the Korean Peninsula."[7]

---

[4]   Ministry of Unification, 2015, p. 25.

[5]   "Kim Jong Un's 2017 New Year's Address," Pyongyang, DPR Korea: The National Committee on North Korea (NCNK), January 2, 2017.

[6]   See the discussion of Kim's objectives in Chapter One.

[7]   Jonathan Cheng, "North Korean Defector Says Kim Jong Un Can't Last," *Wall Street Journal*, January 26, 2017.

Even if Kim Jong-un's days are numbered, peaceful unification is not the only alternative scenario. North Korea could, in theory, evolve in two different directions. First, not only could the Kim family regime collapse, but so could the entire North Korean government, leading to some level of conflict. Second, the Kim family regime could collapse, and a different North Korean leader could take control of the government. Historically, many U.S. and ROK experts on North Korea have considered the first scenario to be the most likely path to unification, even though it would almost certainly involve significant conflict and risk the failure of unification because of North Korean resistance. There has been far less attention paid to the second alternative, although in practice it may well be the preferred choice, offering a more peaceful unification if the successor regime can be persuaded to negotiate a peaceful pathway to merging the two halves of the peninsula.

If a new leader from outside the Kim family takes control of North Korea, he will probably have been personally involved in the North Korean markets and private economy and thus an entrepreneur.[8] It might therefore be possible that he would be more amenable to a Chinese-style set of reforms to the economic system, something that China has urged on North Korea for many years and South Korea has also encouraged.[9] This would move North Korea closer to a free market economy and might establish a reasonable basis for South-North economic cooperation. Over time, the new North Korean government might be willing to discuss meaningful unification with the ROK and move in the direction of a negotiated unification, as opposed to a ROK absorption of the North. Such a pathway to unification is far more likely to avoid serious conflict, although at least some resistance might still be expected once unification occurs because some in North

---

[8] According to several defectors, many senior elites in North Korea have been active as entrepreneurs and merchants, seeking to earn money to better their lives. They are thus pursuing personal profit through trade and industry, the nature of entrepreneurs, although more in the style of Chinese entrepreneurs than Western ones.

[9] "Beijing has called for a Chinese-style opening-up of North Korea's crumbling state-directed economy" ("N. Korea to Set Up Economic Zone on China Border," spacewar.com, June 6, 2011); Na Jeong-ju, "Lee Urges NK to Seek Chinese-Style Economic Reform," *Korea Times*, October 29, 2010.

Korea would be unwilling to change. In contrast to a North Korean government collapse leading to a fairly prompt unification, this kind of unification would likely take many years (perhaps decades) to develop.

It is difficult to believe that new North Korean leaders would be prepared to negotiate for Korean unification without ROK policies in place that would be more favorable to North Korean elites than the existing ones are today. If policies more acceptable to North Korean elites are not in place at the time of an opportunity to pursue negotiated unification, North Korean leaders would certainly demand such changes as part of negotiations. Thus, the unification process would likely be expedited if appropriate South Korean policies were already in place and gave North Korean leaders reason to believe that their interests would be treated seriously in the unification process. It is inconceivable that such an approach to unification could succeed if it called for a de-Ba'athification-like approach to government in a postunification North Korea. Instead, it should be expected that many North Korean elites would want to remain as senior government employees in the unified Korea, and that a relatively forgiving approach would be required in the transitional justice plan. Such a peaceful, negotiated unification would be significantly different from the normal assumptions associated with ROK absorption of North Korea, but also would likely be far less costly to the ROK in terms of both lives lost and financial damages incurred.

## Conditions Appear Ripe to Prepare for Unification

Well before former ROK President Park Geun-hye entered office, she outlined some key aspects of the unification process.[10] And, after entering office, she talked regularly about moving toward Korean unification.[11] Even long before Park, South Korea had significant interest in

---

[10]  Park Geun-Hye, 2011.

[11]  For example, President Park gave a major speech on Korean unification in 2014 at Dresden, Germany. See "Full Text of Park's Speech on N. Korea," *Korea Herald*, March 28, 2014.

unification. For example, in 2009, one prominent defector wrote of North Korea:

> The current crisis, however, stems from the gradually grow-
> ing power of the masses. The state is unable to ration food, the
> market has expanded and the power of individuals is growing to
> an uncontrollable extent. The elite have no choice but to think
> seriously about Chinese-style reform and opening as a way to sur-
> vive. They generally agree that the North is not a normal social-
> ist country, and that Chinese-style reform is not the betrayal of
> socialism the Kim Jong-il regime claims it is.[12]

Now that President Park has been removed from office, her likely successor plans to pursue reconciliation with North Korea, moving toward a peaceful unification. But it is not clear that his efforts will make any more progress in real unification than did Park's efforts.

The potential for change appears to be increasing. A number of North Korean defectors have suggested that substantial portions of the North Korean elite are unhappy with Kim Jong-un. His purges and brutality have made many of his senior personnel very scared of him, while at the same time his leadership is also largely seen as fail-ing, which apparently helps explain Kim Jong-un's paranoia that led to the killing of his elder half-brother, Kim Jong-nam, in February 2017. There is some discussion in North Korea of the flaws in the process that brought Kim Jong-un to power. Reportedly, there was no provision for dynastic succession in either the version of socialism accepted by Kim Il-sung or in the *juche* philosophy developed in North Korea.[13]

Despite these potentially promising signs of intra-elite splits in the North, there does not appear to have been a significant ROK effort to convince North Korean elites that unification would be good for them in anything other than the most vague economic terms. As argued in the two previous sections, regardless of the scenario by which unifica-

---

[12] Kang Chol-hwan, 2009.

[13] *Juche* is a North Korean term that is often translated "self-reliance," but in practice includes a strong component of North Korean nationalism. Interview with a senior North Korean defector, April 2016.

tion occurs, North Korean elites will need to have a positive view about Korean unification; otherwise, unification may never occur or may fail.

It is therefore urgent that the ROK government move to address this issue promptly. It needs to do so by establishing a legal basis for extending amnesty to most North Korean elites upon unification and for planning to continue the role of many elites in the combined Korean government and the combined Korean economy. Korea should also be assembling funds to support the costs of unification to clarify to North Koreans the reality of South Korean planning, consistent with the vision for unification put forward by former ROK President Lee Myung-bak.[14] And the ROK needs to be communicating these efforts into North Korea. Doing so will help facilitate whatever form of unification develops.

---

[14] Former President Lee proposed establishing a $50 billion unification fund derived from tax revenue, but the South Korean people were unwilling to pay that. So, the ROK government turned to collecting voluntary contributions to support unification from companies and the public. See Christian Oliver and Kang Buseong, "S Korea Turns to Donations for Unification Fund," *Financial Times*, November 1, 2011.

# References

Bennett, Bruce W., *Preparing for the Possibility of a North Korean Collapse*, Santa Monica, Calif.: RAND Corporation, RR-331-SRF, 2013. As of April 4, 2017:
http://www.rand.org/pubs/research_reports/RR331.html

Central Intelligence Agency, "Physicians Density," *World Factbook*, undated. As of April 4, 2017:
https://www.cia.gov/library/publications/the-world-factbook/fields/2226.html

Cheng, Jonathan, "North Korean Defector Says Kim Jong Un Can't Last," *Wall Street Journal*, January 26, 2017. As of April 4, 2017:
http://www.wsj.com/articles/
north-korean-defector-says-kim-jong-un-cant-last-1485346155

Choi Song-min, "'Core' Class Urged to Pull the 'Wavering' into Line," *DailyNK*, March 23, 2016. As of April 4, 2017:
http://www.dailynk.com/english/read.php?cataId=nk01500&num=13817

Collins, Robert, *Marked for Life: Songbun, North Korea's Social Classification System*, Washington, D.C.: The Committee for Human Rights in North Korea, June 6, 2012. As of April 4, 2017:
http://www.hrnk.org/uploads/pdfs/HRNK_Songbun_Web.pdf

Demick, Barbara, "Vision on Tunnels Drives N. Korean Defense," *Los Angeles Times*, November 28, 2003. As of April 3, 2017:
http://archive.boston.com/news/world/articles/2003/11/28/
vision_on_tunnels_drives_n_korean_defense/

———, *Nothing to Envy*, New York: Spiegel and Grau, 2009.

"DPR Korea 2008 Population Census: National Report," Pyongyang, DPR Korea: Central Bureau of Statistics, 2009. As of April 4, 2017:
http://unstats.un.org/unsd/demographic/sources/census/wphc/North_Korea/
Final%20national%20census%20report.pdf

Eberstadt, Nicholas, *The End of North Korea*, Washington, D.C.: American Enterprise Institute Press, 1999.

"Full Text of Park's Speech on N. Korea," *Korea Herald*, March 28, 2014. As of April 4, 2017:
http://www.koreaherald.com/view.php?ud=20140328001400

Gale, Alastair, and Kwanwoo Jun, "South Korea's Governors of Northern Provinces Don't—And Never Will—Govern," *Wall Street Journal*, March 17, 2014. As of April 4, 2017:
http://online.wsj.com/article/
SB10001424052702304419104579321810508073546.html

Haggard, Stephan, "Military Promotions in the DPRK," Peterson Institute of International Economics, August 13, 2013. As of April 4, 2017:
https://piie.com/blogs/north-korea-witness-transformation/
military-promotions-dprk

Halpin, Dennis P., "Korea and America, North and South," *NKNews*, March 23, 2015. As of April 4, 2017:
https://www.nknews.org/2015/03/korea-and-america-north-and-south/

Harden, Blaine, *Escape from Camp 14*, New York: Penguin Group, 2012.

"Health > Physicians > Per 1,000 People: Countries Compared," Nationmaster.com, 2003. As of April 4, 2017:
http://www.nationmaster.com/country-info/stats/Health/Physicians/
Per-1,000-people

Herspring, Dale, *Requiem for an Army: The Demise of the East German Military*, Lanham, Md.: Rowman and Littlefield, 1998.

Howard, Young, "North Korean Audience for Open Radio for North Korea," *DailyNK*, February 5, 2006. As of April 4, 2017:
http://www.dailynk.com/english/read.php?cataId=nk01100&num=548

Kang Chol-hwan, "Power Struggle Looms in N. Korea," *Chosun Ilbo*, May 8, 2009. As of April 4, 2017:
http://english.chosun.com/site/data/html_dir/2009/05/08/2009050800706.html

Kim Chae-hwan, "Morale of North Korean Soldiers Drops Despite Visit by Kim Jong Un," *DailyNK*, December 8, 2016. As of April 4, 2017:
http://www.dailynk.com/english/read.php?cataId=nk01500&num=14235

"Kim Jong Un's 2017 New Year's Address," Pyongyang, DPR Korea: The National Committee on North Korea, January 2, 2017. As of April 4, 2017:
http://www.ncnk.org/resources/news-items/
kim-jong-uns-speeches-and-public-statements-1/
kim-jong-uns-2017-new-years-address

Kim Yoo-sung, "Who Goes to North Korea's Top Universities?" *NKNews*, August 26, 2015. As of April 4, 2017:
https://www.nknews.org/2015/08/who-goes-to-north-koreas-top-universities/

*Korea North: Energy Policy, Laws and Regulation Handbook: Strategic Information and Developments,* Vol. 1 (Strategic Information and Developments), Washington, D.C.: International Business Publications, USA, March 3, 2008.

Ministry of Unification, *Initiative for Korean Unification*, Seoul, October 2015.

"N. Korea Purging Descendants of Anti-Japanese Guerrillas: Defector," *Korea Herald*, January 27, 2017. As of April 4, 2017:
http://www.koreaherald.com/view.php?ud=20170127000058

"N. Korea to Set Up Economic Zone on China Border," spacewar.com, June 6, 2011. As of April 4, 2017:
http://www.spacewar.com/reports/N_Korea_to_set_up_economic_zone_on_China_border_999.html

Na Jeong-ju, "Lee Urges NK to Seek Chinese-Style Economic Reform," *Korea Times*, October 29, 2010. As of April 4, 2017:
http://www.koreatimes.co.kr/www/news/nation/2016/10/116_75416.html

Oliver, Christian, and Kang Buseong, "S Korea Turns to Donations for Unification Fund," *Financial Times*, November 1, 2011. As of April 4, 2017:
https://www.ft.com/content/17e35d96-0466-11e1-ac2a-00144feabdc0

Park Geun-hye, "A New Kind of Korea: Building Trust Between Seoul and Pyongyang," *Foreign Affairs,* September/October 2011. As of April 4, 2017:
https://www.foreignaffairs.com/articles/northeast-asia/2011-09-01/new-kind-korea

"Pyongyang Now More Than One-Third Smaller; Food Shortage Issues Suspected," *Asahi Shimbun*, July 17, 2010.

Republic of Korea, Ministry of National Defense, *2014 Defense White Paper*, January 6, 2015.

ROK—*See* Republic of Korea.

Scarlatoiu, Greg, Jana Johnson, and Miran Song, "Re-Defection to North Korea: Exaggeration or the Beginning of a Trend?" *NKNews*, January 24, 2013. As of April 4, 2017:
http://www.NKNews.Org/2013/01/Re-Defection-to-North-Korea-Exaggeration-or-the-Beginning-of-a-Trend/

Sissons, Miranda, and Abdulrazzaq Al-Saiedi, "Iraq's de-Baathification Still Haunts the Country," *Al Jazeera*, March 12, 2013. As of April 4, 2017:
http://www.aljazeera.com/indepth/opinion/2013/03/201331055338463426.html

Vollertsen, Norbert, "A Depraved Society We Can't Ignore," *American Enterprise*, July/August 2005. As of April 4, 2017:
https://www.highbeam.com/doc/1G1-133755168.html

White House, Office of the Press Secretary, "Joint Declaration in Commemoration of the 60th Anniversary of the Alliance Between the Republic of Korea and the United States of America," Washington D.C., May 2013. As of April 4, 2017: https://obamawhitehouse.archives.gov/the-press-office/2013/05/07/ joint-declaration-commemoration-60th-anniversary-alliance-between-republ